*His darkness
Led to light.*

Introspectrum

by R.Sen

iiPUBLISHING

Introspectrum
Copyright © 2020 by R.Sen

Copyright notice
All rights reserved. No part of this book may be reproduced in any form or by any electronic or mechanical means, including information storage and retrieval systems, without permission in writing from the author or publisher, except for the use of brief quotations in a book review.

Cover design and illustrations by Nupur Nair

ISBN: 978-1-7362167-3-6

Printed in the United States of America

iiPUBLISHING
New York, NY
www.toniiinc.com

from dark to light...

DARK
page 1

PENUMBRA
page 24

LIGHT
page 46

Welcome to my dark and my light
Filled with my grim and my delight
A depiction of my daily plight
In it, you will find day and night
This process of turning my darkness bright.

DARK

to be blinded from your own light.

...as mystical as it was
We blocked each other's light
I now lie here lost in the shadows we composed
Not understanding who I am, what I am,
Nor what is love
Only lightless answers for the questions I pose.

It's expired
That love which I so greatly desired
Invested my whole soul
Into the storybook romance it inspired
That ended *Unhappily ever after.*

Expiration

Anxiety comes
As I lose this love
Because with it
I lose myself and my soul
But without it I'm still incomplete
It's a successful defeat
Ironically, I die while breathing
I never knew you could love someone
And also hate someone so clearly
I fear the dark without your light
And the light sans your darkness.

Anxiety

While I make you my world
You break me with the weight of yours
And leave me broken in fragments.

Unbreakable

It's like I died without you
An embalmed existence

A forever eulogy spoken while I'm remembering
Every word of our memories

Tears embroider my casket
And my corpse is clothed in sadness

How does one live after death?
I am consistently asking

Life removed of reason and passion

This death I live,
No burial.

Funeral

Her once Kohl-rimmed eyes
Brim with black streams from thinking of you
Remembering your existence and its absence
Made death cuddle her soul when she realized you
    were never hers in the way she was yours

You possessed what she could never receive
And she desired what you could not give

Your actions etched "Rest in Peace" on her forehead

In my body lies a women who is intangibly and
    invariably ruined.

RIP

I thought to myself,
"I should keep drinking until the pain of him never returning is gone..."

Turns out, there's not enough alcohol.

Libations

Tell me how to escape this cage
I'm not normal...

It's not normal to be captured in love this way

I cannot escape my yearn for your embrace

Yet, you are a mere skeleton of the flesh I once knew
But I am prisoner of the thought of what was
        once you...once us...once true

Hoping somehow I can unshackle the lies found
In the curve of my frown

My prince was the dragon
With a rib cage like a dungeon
I, a princess with filth and shit on her crown

I have imprisoned myself in you
I am stuck...
I am lost...
I am reaching...

I need to leave...
I need to run...
I need to exit...

Please release me.

Prisoner

Stare at the moon long enough and you will become a slave to it's beauty

You are my moon.

Lunar

I'm connected to you
I find no one like you
There are so many others
But like you?
There is no other.

No Other

You were
Warm,
Orange,
Cozy,
Silent,
Peaceful,
And my comfort.

Until you showed me what fires do.

Fire You Are

Memories remain in my veins
With no pulse to clear them out
No rhythm for life's existence
Silent cavity behind rib cages
Imprison absent palpitations

Heartless

How do you love someone that was never really there?

I had never met you before,
But it was like picking up a book and opening to the
    page I left off
Your dimpled smile and vibrant personality fit so well
Into my faux grin and battered insecurities
But...
I knew...just like I know now
That we were meant to meet

So the taste and the consumption of your toxicity
Still did not prevent me
From knowing we belonged together

I knew...just like I know now
Despite the darkness that existed in our sunlight
And the eclipse behind your lips
Filled with fables

I still knew...just like I know now

That the pain, abuse, and deceit
Did not imvalidate our destiny to meet and be together
Happy or unhappily
It doesn't matter because
I knew...just like I know now

That I probably don't know what's good for me

I am just hoping you do.

What do I know?

You lied to me
In saying those three words
That you knew would mean everything to me
Yet, nothing to you.

Deception

Did I ever have all of the pieces to solve your puzzle?

Did you ever love me
Or was I just the hand you were dealt?

Was I a queen or a pawn on your chess board?

Did my dice ever roll and land on pairs?

Were we just a game?

Games

All I have ever wanted is you
And then while having you, I still do
I am lost without you
And never found with you
Why be with me
But not *with me?*
Why feed me hunger,
Let me drink thirst,
And live dead?

Paradox

    ...yet, I still love you with every cell in my body.

I never knew that my love could be so limitless
That I lose my sense of self.

Selfless

It's better off I don't know
It makes it easier to forget you
It's better off I remember the pain
And destruction you caused
Than the warmth and joy once upon a time
~~It's better off this way~~
I am better off this way.

Better Off

I have reached a point of emptiness
I never thought I would get to this point
But, here I am...
At the point of no return
Things you used to say and do
Once filled my heart with warmth and joy
Now are mundane and habitual
Charm is lackluster
Warmth is lukewarm
There is nothing left to find in you
So I'm left trying to find everything in me.

Empty

If you jump
I jump
If you weep
I weep
If you love
I love
If you need
I leave
If you express
I repress
If you care
I accept
If I...
Never happens.

Conditioning

I'm going around in circles thinking...

I'm addicted to wasting my time

I give away my energy
Relentless...ly

Undeserving of it,
You are not right...*for me*

But I think you are

You are a hurricane
So why do I only see sunshine?

I'm not fine
This complication is all mine
And the reality is simple:

I'm much too addicted to wasting my time.

Overthinking

There was beauty in my light within your darkness
You did not savor my presence
But you will crave it in my absence.

Gone

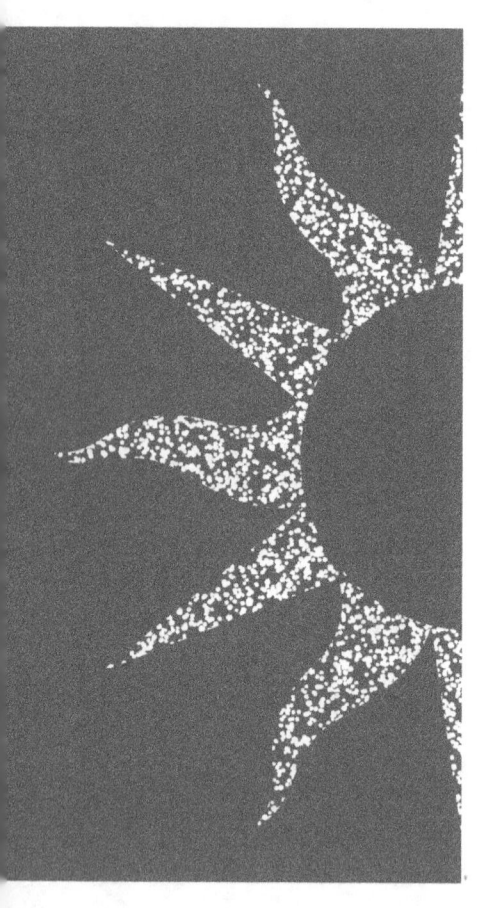

PENUMBRA

Lifting one's veil of darkness to discover
the light and truth of one's hearts.

I am worthy of love
Love of self
Love of mind
Love of heart
This is how I now know...

No more strings
I free myself of your control
Liberated by self-love and joy
I am no longer your marionette
I am real.

Puppeteer

What's wrong with me to think there was a "we" when there was never a "me"?

You disposed of me
Pushed me down at any excuse, just to break-away
You were mean to me
Yet somehow you still mean the world to me
I don't understand why my heart could not see
What my mind could see
Why did loving you mean I stopped loving me?
I was trapped and confused
Blind sighted, used, and abused
Yet every time you attacked
I was the one who kept crawling back
Was I really that desperate
To not be alone with my thoughts?

The Irony

Cross my heart and hope to die
Hope you never cross my mind.

I never felt the fires of hatred in my heart
Then, I met you and faced the flames
You tested my tolerance with deception
Then I realized
How much of a sour taste
You left on my sugar frosted breath.

Unworthy

I don't need your validation to understand my worth
I just needed your validation that my heart had worth.

Invalid

A fool for love is a fool for pain
In the end...
Your loss, my gain.

The Narc

You were so sweet entering my lips
I got consumed in the richness of your taste
Then...
You spilled and all of your sticky remnants
Invited dirt, dust, rubbish, and unwanted disaster
In my life.

Just A Honey

The tears streamed down my face
But my world did not shatter
I saw your picture today
It didn't make my heart drop
It didn't well my eyes
It is like footprints in my memories,
That have led to my growth.

Growth

I recoil into silence
My presence drifts away
I'm not an important factor in your story
Never was
Just happenstance
But I do play a major role in my own though
And I know what I deserve
So now I am holding the pen
Because owning who you are is the greatest strength,
It is the ink
I am no longer narrated by what you think.

The Protagonist

You were my sunlight, air, and water
Never would I have thought
You were the one who would break me
Only to help me bloom on my own.

Flower

I died for a minute.
My world was filled with darkness and decay
That's when you found me and made me realize
Even decay creates nutrients to sustain life
And from those nutrients, here I stand, alive.

Decay

How can I be so unattached in intimate situations? Well, that's what happens when you have no more heart left to break.

Remedy by Default

It wasn't my fault
Just bad business.
I expected great return
From too much investment.

Asset

Sometimes my will to live
Hangs on to the threads of my dress
That has been left with little give
So lost in my own thoughts, so lost in the stress.

Seam-stressed

Is darkness an appealing quality?
I have a lot of it
From my melanin to my mind
I'm pigmented in 60 shades of darkness
But, I am also light.

Duality

My Heart is very broken
But also full
I stay up nights alone
But I'm loved in the morning
Fighting my demons
Against my angels
My thoughts are a process
Balancing my heart
I do not sleep
But, I dream
The battle in my mind
Is clear but confusing
In the distance,

A vanishing solution.

Contrast

I don't know what I believe anymore.
Sometimes in my most blissful state
I look around and wonder
Am I truly happy or am I just settling?
Is there truly a blissful state?
Or is it just accepting what you have?
Am I addicted to sadness and darkness?
Was my darkness ever a reality
Is happiness just a protective veil?
Nothing is real
Not even how I Feel.

Addict

Empty, vacant dreams
Cold, indifferent hearts
Faux eagerness
Impassionate motives
Unnoticed beauty above us
Stars twinkling in vain
While identities are lost
In a somber routine.

Numb Life

I wish my life wasn't like my old broken camera lens,
Every shot, a blurry scene
Leaving me in an unclear reality
Not knowing what's good or bad for me.

The Photo Lens

You control your perspective
The dove can be a representation of
Beauty
Innocence
And grace

OR

It can be another damn bird that might shit on you

Your view is up to you.

Perspective

A wilted rose-beautiful and old
A springtime rose-young and hopeful
The both of them are full of promise
The plucked rose, the one you hold
So fragrant.
So beautiful.
A combination of both.
Which one do you choose to think about?
The rose that was or the bud to be?

Roses

I use to see myself in you
Now I see myself in me
I loved you with every ounce of my soul
I supported you with every bone in my body
I thought of you with every cell of my mind
I breathed you with every molecule of me
Now, I only see me
I am beautiful
I am smart
I am sweet
I am strong
I am a light in your darkness
I love you with all of my heart
Believe in us with all of my soul
We are light.

I know my Worth

Goodbyes are always difficult
Because saying goodbye means letting go
But it is time...

Goodbye

LIGHT

to illuminate from within and discover the love of self.

Adjust yourself and love yourself
Before you love someone else
It was a blessing
To lose myself in you
To discover who I was meant to be
And now I stand here illuminated
Like a singular sunbeam peaking through the blinds
Having experienced dusk to bring forth my dawn
And now I shine.

Harsh words, soft voice
Stone cold melts into a rolling waterfall
Tears streaming down her stoic face
Bending down to her knees
She gives in to release
And finds peace.

You are glitter, never stop sparkling.

I do this for me
I've never done it that way.

Just remember even a diamond started off as coal
There is no such thing as an unattainable goal
You are the creator and destroyer of your own destiny
Keep your dreams high, and you will land them
Successfully.

I am either the Sun blazing with warmth
That melts your soul with joy,
Or an ice storm that will freeze you to your soul
And pierce it with pain

Choose your season.

You break
You bleed
You cry
You rage
You get up
You wake up
You find another way.

Time is of the essence
It is the greatest gift
It is the grandest show of love
When you use it wisely

Know this:
If time is of the essence,
Then, you are of the necessity
If time is a gift,
Then, you are a blessing
If time is a show of love
My dear, then, you are a timeless romance.

The world has crashed around me
Chaos, madness, hatred everywhere
But I have learned to remain calm
With deep breaths filling my lungs
I remain calm
And it is my calm that makes me rise
I rise
I will rise
I have always risen.

Life is now a beautiful dream.

Today, I woke up smiling
I bid my past farewell
Lifted, awakened from my deep slumber
Light on my feet after so long
Floating lighter than a feather
Taking steps forward with no need to go backwards
The shackles of darkness are gone
Finally...
The sun and I rise together as one
I have made it,
My dawn.

Dawn

Afterword

To anyone who resonated with my pain, heartbreak, and anguish while reading this; to anyone who can relate to my journey of self-love; and to all of my dear, sweet readers:

This is not a poem. This is a message and a call to action to anyone who can relate to the words written here. These poems were written in a state of raw emotion. They were written in the midst and after a volatile and painful relationship. The aftermath of such a relationship brought pain, depression, and low self worth but, through reflection it also led to a better version of myself. I did not realize what I was experiencing while I was in the relationship, but I knew I did not feel like myself in it. I was genuinely unhappy, exhausted emotionally, and my self-confidence was at rock bottom.

Interestingly enough, I still thought I was in love, despite, the behaviors and treatment that caused me to feel that way. I stuck around for years, unabashedly hopeful. Hoping things will change, hoping the way I felt about him would somehow be reciprocated, and hoping that any decent treatment I received would be a permanent change, as I longed for him to recognize my value.

I was wrong. Things never changed, and eventually my patience ran out, so I left, and I never looked back. Instead, I ran into my reflection.

I know that these poems may resonate with many of you struggling to understand the difficulties of love.

Well, I am here as a testimony, letting you know that love never drains you; it never makes you lose yourself; and never makes you fall out of love with your reflection. Love enhances, grows, and illuminates you out of your darkest feelings. Love beautifies and amplifies your greatness.

If you believe that you are in love, and your loved one makes you feel unworthy and unlovable more than confident and appreciated, please listen to me when I say "that ain't it." Please let my words and my story fuel and empower you to walk away. You are worthy of love that makes you feel worthy.

This is your reminder, my beautiful king, queen, and everyone in between: Know your worth. Know yourself. And NEVER let Someone else eclipse your light. Shine permanently.

Gratitude

Gratitude /ˈgradə͵t(y)o͞od/: *to show appreciation for the things that give you life.*

I wanted to make this short and general, but my heart is filled with several emotions as this book has come to be, so goodbye formalities:

To my readers, I am so honored and humbled to be able to share my journey with you. Thank you so much for reading picking this book to explore its pages.

To my supporters everywhere, thank you for showing me my words mean something to someone. I often battle with my worthiness and potential, but your consistent support has helped with my journey, my growth and the evolution of who I am becoming. This book is for you and because of you. I found strength in continuing my journey, knowing that I am not alone. I thank you for being there for me.

To my publisher (ii Publishing), thank you for taking a chance on what I have to say and helping to make my dream manifest into reality. And to the entire poetic community, thank you for embracing and accepting me in this amazing creative space. Without your support, inspiration, and guidance, I would have never evolved - not only as a poet, but as a person too. Poetry has always been my outlet and channel of expression, but sharing it with others has been the therapy I have needed for years. I am so thrilled that my expression has found a home in you.

To my parents, my biggest supporters, thank you for coming to the USA to pursue your dreams. This opened so many doors for my brother and I to pursue ours. You endured so much so that we wouldn't have to. It is an honor to follow your example in everything I do. Additionally, I am specifically grateful to have parents who have supported me and accepted me as I am. It has truly made the difference in my life.

Similarly, a huge thank you to my aunts and uncles (some of who are like a second set of parents for me). And to my brother in California and my brothers and sisters in India and New Zealand, thank you for always being a shoulder to lean on and always a phone call away. In this same breath, I want to express my sincere appreciation to all of my friends. You have been my chosen family. I am so grateful to have your support and love.

To my maternal and paternal grandparents, who have passed away, thank you for offering your wisdom, guidance and support while you were alive. I know you continue to guide me and motivate me spiritually as I continue to pursue my goals. Rest in peace, and I hope that I am making you proud.

Finally, thank you again to everyone who has picked this book up and read its words. You are one of the most important reason why this book exists at all. I share this in hopes that at least one of you are changed for the better because of my words.

Much love, positive energy, and gratitude to all of you.

R.Sen is a New Jersey based spoken word artist, writer, and poet who found love for writing at the age 16. She has since used this passion in many readings/performances, both online and in-person, throughout the COVID-19 pandemic. It was during this time of uncertainty, that she found the power in her voice to speak her words. Her belief in poetry being therapy and the feedback from peers motivated her to begin composing her first collection, so that she can not only empower her own life, but the lives of others around the world. With love as a focus topic, her work is taylored to resonate with those who have struggled in life with heartbreak, loss, and self worth. R.Sen writes for her readers to find healing, strength, hope, and ultimately, self love by guiding them with poetry through her own personal journey.

To stay in touch with her and her work, you can follow her on Instagram at @r.sen_thepoet.

www.ingramcontent.com/pod-product-compliance
Lightning Source LLC
Chambersburg PA
CBHW072207100526
44589CB00015B/2412